There was a little girl named Chrissy.

She loved playing with her two sissy's.

They played with their barbies and video games.

They loved dressing up to look the same.

They played outside and rode their bikes.

They loved going to the trails to hike.

They loved dancing to a musical beat.

They loved to ice skate and skate in the street.

They sometimes fought about their toy's.

They never fought over the boy's.

They loved to play school and house.

And their mom once chased away a mouse.

Their dad bought them hamster's, iguana's, and fish.

And their mom always made a tasty food dish.

They loved going to school and making new friends.

And they didn't like it when Summer came to an end.

They loved to play make believe.

And was always striving to achieve.

They loved to do their best at everything.

They also loved to sing.

They loved to paint and draw.

They loved to play the card game war.

The girls loved Sunday dinner with grandma and grandpa.

And they loved making wishes on a star.

They believed in Santa Clause and the Easter Bunny.

And their dad was always acting so funny.

They loved going to the beach and the park.

They loved playing hide and seek.

They couldn't wait until the end of the week.

Their mom ordered pizzas and snacks.

Their dad rode them on piggyback.

They we're just three sisters who we're also best friend's.

Made in the USA
Las Vegas, NV
19 March 2025